My Religion and Me

We are CHRISTIANS

Philip Blake

FRANKLIN WATTS
LONDON • SYDNEY

Franklin Watts
338 Euston Road
London, NW1 3BH

Franklin Watts Australia
Level 17/207 Kent Street
Sydney, NSW 2000

Series designed and created for Franklin Watts by Storeybooks.

Acknowledgements
The Publisher would like to thank Annie Measures, Roger Verrall,
Cameron Morris, Oliver Taylor-Meade and Marietta as well as St Mary's Church,
Banbury for their help in producing this book.

Faith advisor Martin Ganeri

Photo credits:
Chsch/Dreamstime: front cover br. Pooterjon/Dreamstime: front cover bl. I stock pp 4,
5(bottom), 17(bottom), 18(bottom left and right), 19(top), 21, 23, 25(top) and 31;
Tudor Photography pp 1(bottom), 3(bottom left), 7(left), 16, 17(top), 18(top),
19(bottom), 26, 27 and p30. Every attempt has been made to clear copyright. Should
there be any inadvertent omission please apply to the publisher for rectification.

Additional photographs were supplied by the children featured in the book.

Dewey number: 230

ISBN: 978 1 4451 3825 1

Printed in Malaysia

Franklin Watts is a division of Hachette Children's Books,
an Hachette UK company. www.hachette.co.uk

Note:
The opinions expressed in this book are personal to the children
we talked to and all opinions are subjective and can vary.

Contents

Words in **bold** can be found in the glossary

What is Christianity?

▲ *A mosaic image of Jesus from an early Christian church.*

Christianity is a religion that began about 2,000 years ago with the teachings of Jesus. Today, millions of people around the world are Christians.

What Christians believe

Christians are people who follow the teachings of Jesus Christ. They believe that Jesus is the Son of God and that his mother, Mary, was still a virgin when he was born. Jesus grew up in Palestine in the eastern Mediterranean (modern Israel). He preached in the area around the Sea of Galilee. Christians believe that Jesus was crucified, that he rose from the dead and joined his father in heaven. Christians believe that if they have faith in Jesus, are sorry for their sins and lead a good life, their **souls** will go to heaven and live on after they die.

The **Bible**, Christianity's holy book, tells how the Angel Gabriel visited Mary. Gabriel told her that, although she was still a virgin, she would give birth to God's son. As the mother of Jesus, Mary is revered by Christians, especially Catholics.

This is a statue of ▶
the Virgin Mary.

Worshipping God

Christians usually go to church on Sundays. There they worship God by singing hymns, saying prayers and listening to readings from the Bible. A church leader called a priest, pastor, vicar or minister leads these services. He or she teaches people about Christianity and leads rituals such as Holy Communion.

◀ *Christians worship in an Anglican church. They stand to sing a hymn.*

Kinds of church

There are many different kinds of Christian church, including Roman Catholic, Anglican (also called Episcopalian or Church of England) and Baptist. The churches are quite different from each other in the way their followers worship and in their buildings. For example, many Catholic churches are often very ornate, with lots of pictures and statues, while Baptist churches are usually much plainer. But all Christians share many of the same beliefs about God and Jesus.

▼ *After hurricane Katrina struck the USA in 2005, some churches were destroyed. One church put up a canvas roof to shelter worshippers.*

Christianity Around the World

Christians live all over the world, but some places are home to more Christians than others. For example, in North America, Europe and parts of Africa most religious people follow Christianity.

Christians in North America

In North America, most Christians are **Protestants**. This means that they are not Catholic. Protestant churches include Baptists, Methodists and **Episcopalians** or Anglicans.

My name is **Cameron** and I am 11 years old. I am a Baptist from Pennsylvania, in the United States of America and I live in the city of Philadelphia. I like living there because it is very big and there is always something new to do with my friends.

Christians in Europe

In northern Europe there are also many Protestants. For example in England a lot of people are Anglican. Some Central European countries, such as Poland, have mainly Catholics, while in Russia and eastern Europe there are many Orthodox Christian Churches.

Christians in Africa

There are many Christians in Africa. Thousands of "new" Churches have been founded there in the last few decades.

I am **Oliver** and I am 11 years old. I am a Roman Catholic. I live with my parents and my brother, Hugo, in Cahirsiveen. Cahirsiveen is a small town on the south west coast of Ireland, it is close to beautiful mountains and the sea, which are great for doing things outdoors and having lots of fun with my friends.

I am **Marietta**. I am 12 years old and I live in Bochnia in Poland. Bochnia is a small town not far from Cracow. I am a Catholic and I am in my last year of primary school. I have a younger brother who is six years old and a sister who is much older – she is 17. I play a lot of football and I like listening to music.

My name is **Annie** and I am ten years old. I live in Banbury, which is in England. I go to school at St Mary's Primary School, which is a Church of England school. My school is near to where I live. I live with my mother and father, sister and three brothers. My brothers are all 13 years old because they are triplets. We are all Anglicans.

In this book, four children share their experiences of Christian faith. It is important to remember that other Christians will have different opinions and experiences of their own faith.

A Christian Life
Marietta's story

▲ *I read all about Jesus in the Bible.*

Annie says:
I think Jesus was a very kind man. He wanted people to be nice to others.

For me, being a Christian is not just about going to church. It is about being good in what I do every day, too. In the Bible, Jesus spends a lot of time teaching us how to live a good, Christian life.

Love your neighbour

Jesus told his followers to "love your neighbour". By "neighbour", I think he meant anyone you might come across – even someone you don't like or might think of as an enemy. Jesus told us to be helpful, **considerate** and kind. He also discouraged his followers from worrying too much about things such as clothes and food. Jesus also said that if you have a lot of money, you should give away most of it to the poor. I think respect for others also means telling the truth and not stealing.

Living in peace

The religious teachers of Jesus' time said it was wrong to kill people, but Jesus said this was not enough. Christians should avoid violence completely.

They should try not to even have violent thoughts. Christians should help everyone to live together peacefully.

I pray in front of the altar at our church.

Forgiveness

Jesus knew that we all can make mistakes and sometimes do wrong – even if we do not mean to. He forgave us our sins and mistakes, and told us to be forgiving to other people, too. He taught his followers the Lord's Prayer, which asks God to forgive us, and says that we should be forgiving in our turn.

The Lord's Prayer
Our Father, who art in heaven
Hallowed be thy Name
Thy **kingdom** come
Thy will be done, on earth as it is in heaven
Give us this day our daily bread
And forgive us our **trespasses**, as we forgive
    those who trespass against us
Lead us not into **temptation**
But deliver us from evil.

Amen

Cameron says:
Jesus was a kind, caring person who wants us all to love one another.

I use a special string of beads called a rosary to count my prayers.

Oliver says:
Jesus was forgiving and understanding. He helped the poor and he treated all people as equals.

9

At My Church
Marietta's story

▲ *I follow the service in my prayer book.*

My church is a large, very old building. From the outside, you can tell it is a church because of the big cross on the roof. Inside there are all kinds of things to remind us about God and the story of Jesus that is so important to us.

A special place

Church is a very special place for me. I enjoy singing hymns from my song book and listening to the priest as he explains about God and about how we should all be good Christians. I like to go to church when it is empty so that I can sit quietly, say a prayer, and think about things in silence.

◀ *The front of my church has a cross at the very top.*

Cameron says:
I go to a small church. We help homeless people and hold events to raise money to give to charities.

The Virgin Mary

There are paintings and statues of the **saints** and of scenes and people from the Bible around our church. My favourite is a painting of Mary. I think it is a beautiful picture. Mary is very special to us because she was the mother of Jesus.

The Stations of the Cross

On the walls of my church there are also paintings of Jesus' **crucifixion**. They are called the **Stations of the Cross** and show Jesus on his journey to Calvary, the place where he was crucified. There are 14 pictures altogether, and they tell the whole story of the crucifixion. At Easter time, we stand and pray in front of each picture in turn, to help us understand what happened to Jesus.

▲ A beautiful altar in my church.

◀ One of the Stations of the Cross.

Annie says:
My church has paintings of Jesus, Mary, and the saints. They remind us that it is a holy place.

Oliver says:
On one wall of my church, an explanation of the **Gospel** for children helps us to understand the importance of **Mass**.

Sunday School
Cameron's story

Every Sunday before church I go to Sunday school. In Sunday school I join children who are about the same age as me and we learn all about God and Jesus and the Bible. As well as getting to know the stories in the Bible, we learn what the Bible teaches us about our lives and how to use its lessons in everyday situations.

My Sunday school

My Sunday school is upstairs in our church. It is quite large, and is heated and air-conditioned. There are several classrooms, which are a bit like the ones at school except they are a lot smaller.

▼ *I am sitting in my Sunday school room at our church.*

Annie says:
We learn about Jesus by listening to the stories our Sunday school teacher tells us.

▲ *I like playing the drums and I am going to be a youth drummer in our new praise ensemble. I have also been in the youth choir since I was seven years old.*

▼ *This rug in our Sunday school room shows the Bible story of Noah's Ark.*

Our classes

Different age groups go to different classes at Sunday school. Each age group has different activities but every class reads and learns about the Bible. We also do things such as painting and drawing and making things like Christmas and Easter cards for our friends and family. The younger children get prizes or stickers when they do their work well or answer questions correctly.

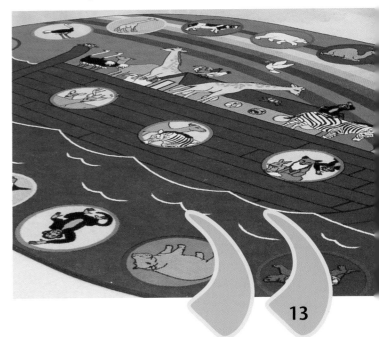

At Prayer
Cameron's story

In the sanctuary area of our church there is a large cross above the altar.

Annie says:
When I pray, I kneel down to show that I respect and love God.

Prayer is really important because it is when I talk to God and ask him to help me and other people. Jesus showed that he cared a lot about children, so I think it is just as important for children to pray as it is for adults. I pray at home, at school and at church and I believe that God answers my prayers.

In my prayers

When I pray I usually pray for my family and friends and sometimes for other people I know. I also pray for people who have done bad things and who need God's help and forgiveness. I ask God for things for myself too.

The Lord's Prayer

Every day at school I say the Lord's Prayer, which begins, "Our Father, who art in Heaven" (see page 9). The Lord's Prayer is very special because it was the prayer that Jesus taught his **disciples**. It asks God to forgive us for all the bad things we have done.

Concentrating

I think people should concentrate when they pray. I try hard not to get my thoughts mixed up during prayers – it would be like giving God a television that changes channels every few seconds.

Marietta says:
The Lord's Prayer was the very first prayer I learned. I still say it every morning and evening at home.

▲ *The words of the Lord's Prayer are displayed on one of the walls of my church.*

▼ *I act as **acolyte**, helping with the candles on the altar.*

Oliver says:
I pray to say thank you to God for the good things that have happened in my life.

The Bible

Annie's story

The Bible is really important because it tells us about Jesus and his teachings. Every Sunday we have Bible readings in church and the priest explains what the Bible's teachings mean for us today. I also read the Bible at home and at school.

▲ *Sometimes at a church service I read to everyone from the big Bible.*

Reading about Jesus

The Bible tells us everything about the life of Jesus – it explains how he was born and grew up with Mary and **Joseph**, and describes what he taught and preached. It also tells us how he was crucified, and how he rose again from the dead.

16

> *Oliver says:*
> I like the Bible story of the loaves and fishes. It tells how Jesus was able to feed many people with a small amount of food.

The first Christians

The Bible also tells the stories of the first Christians. These people spread the faith and some of them travelled a lot, preaching as they went. I find it interesting to read about how they founded churches around the Mediterranean. They even reached Rome in Italy, where one of them, St Peter, became the first leader of the Roman Catholic Church.

▲ At a church service, our vicar reads a passage from the Bible and he talks to us about what the passage means.

> *Marietta says:*
> I read the Bible at home and at school. It tells Christians everything they need to know about Jesus.

The Old Testament

Some of my favourite Bible stories are in the Old Testament – the stories of the Jewish people before the time of Jesus. I like the stories of Noah, who saved his family from the great flood, and Moses, who led his people to their promised homeland. The Old Testament also tells us about the **prophets**. They are men who predicted that one day Jesus would come to save all our souls.

◀ Stained-glass windows illustrate Bible stories. This is a picture of Noah with his ark.

Sadness and Joy
Annie's story

Easter is the most important time of the year for Christians and our family always goes to church. The services around Easter remember both the sadness of Jesus' crucifixion and the joy when he rose from the dead three days later.

Holy Week
The week before Easter is called **Holy Week**. At our church the services are very serious, as we remember how Jesus came to be crucified. We are given little palm-leaf crosses to remind us about the story in the Bible about how, when Jesus rode into Jerusalem, the crowd welcomed him by tearing down palm leaves and laying them on the road in front of him.

◀ *Jesus on the cross.*

Marietta says:
After Palm Sunday our church is dark and sad. People are waiting for the day of Christ's **resurrection**.

◀ *Palm crosses mark Palm Sunday, the day when Jesus rode into Jerusalem before he was crucified.*

◀ *This tomb in Israel was made around the same time that Jesus was crucified, and he was buried in a similar tomb.*

Jesus was crucified on a Friday and his body was put in a tomb. The following Sunday, some of his friends found the tomb was empty. Christian's believe Jesus had risen from the dead.

▼ *I am about to remove the wrapping from my chocolate Easter egg.*

Easter eggs remind Christians of new birth and new life. Jesus was "reborn" when he rose from the dead on Easter Sunday.

Cameron says:
On Easter Sunday we go to a sunrise service and afterwards have a special Easter breakfast. Sometimes there is a play about the Easter story.

Easter Sunday

I like Easter Sunday because the mood is much more joyful. I go to the special service at our church. The vicar explains how Jesus rose from the dead. I listen to the readings from the Bible. They tell the story of Jesus' resurrection and explain how he came to bring us **salvation** and joy. We all sing lively hymns that are full of hope.

Easter eggs

I especially enjoy the chocolate eggs that I'm given at Easter. We always have an Easter egg hunt when I join the other children from our church to look for the eggs that our vicar has hidden. Everyone hopes to find an egg. My parents usually give me a big chocolate egg, too.

Special Journeys
Oliver's story

▲ This is me, outside our church.

Marietta says:
The shrine of the Virgin Mary of Jasna Gorna at Czestochowa is the most popular pilgrimage place in Poland.

Some people from our church have been on journeys to special places to do with our religion. A few have been to Rome. Others have travelled to places that have links with some of the Christian saints. These special journeys are called pilgrimages and many people find that going on a pilgrimage helps to strengthen their faith in God.

Going to the Vatican

The Vatican, near Rome, is important to all Catholics because it is where the **Pope** lives and leads the church. People who make the pilgrimage to the Vatican gather in the huge square in front of St Peter's church. While they are there, they attend Mass and say special prayers for their loved ones.

Receiving a blessing

At Easter, the pilgrims watch as the Pope appears on his balcony to bless everyone – those in the square at the Vatican and the rest of the world.

▲ *Large crowds of pilgrims gather in St Peter's Square, at the Vatican, at the times when the Pope is about to give his blessing.*

Annie says:
Anglicans in Great Britain sometimes make pilgrimages to the shrine of Our Lady at Walsingham, or to Canterbury Cathedral, the most important Anglican church.

Sometimes, people are able to meet the Pope and receive the Holy Father's blessing personally.

Visiting a shrine

Places that have a link with one of the saints or house their relics are known as shrines. Many people make pilgrimages to these places – often because miracles have happened there. For example, at the shrine of St Bernadette at Lourdes, many sick people have been healed of their illnesses. Not only sick people go there – others make the pilgrimage and say a special prayer for people they know who are ill.

▲ *People light candles at shrines like Lourdes. They say that the burning candle continues their prayers.*

21

A New Baby
Oliver's story

All Catholic children are baptized **when they are babies, to show that they are members of the church.** I can't remember my own baptism, but I can remember when my baby brother was baptized at our church about four years ago – he was one year old.

God-parents

For every baptism, several adults – usually two or three – agree to be the child's **God-parents.** God-parents need to be kind people who will take care of the child's spiritual life. They make sure that he or she goes to church and also answer any questions he or she has about religion.

At the ceremony

As well as my parents and me and my brother's God-parents, lots of our relatives and friends came to the ceremony. During the ceremony my family stood around the font and the priest asked my parents and my brother's God-parents questions about their belief in God.

▲ *I still have the presents I was given at my baptism.*

Cameron says:
In my church people are usually baptized when they are older, so I have not been baptized yet.

Promises for the future

Then the priest explained the meaning of baptism to us all, saying that it was a way of welcoming my brother into the church. I watched the priest as he blessed my brother, making the **sign of the cross** on his forehead with holy water. The God-parents promised to guide my brother, and my mother lit a candle as a sign of the guiding light of Jesus in our lives. At the end of the ceremony the priest blessed us all.

Annie says:
In the Anglican church we call baptism christening. The vicar blesses the baby by pouring holy water over his or her head.

In Jesus' time, John the Baptist baptized people by dipping them in the River Jordan. When they came out of the water they were "reborn" spiritually. Today, baptism is a ceremony using water that marks the beginning of a person's life as a Christian.

The celebration meal

After the ceremony we all went out to dinner. We had a special cake with my brother's name iced on top. My brother sat in a high chair at one end of the table. His God-parents gave him a beautiful Bible that he can use when he is older.

▲ *God-parents often give their God-children a copy of the Bible.*

Marietta says:
In our church the priest makes the sign of the cross on the baby's head with special holy oil.

▼ *My brother was baptized at a font like this one.*

23

First Communion
Oliver's story

▲ *Making my first Holy Communion was very important to me.*

Cameron says:
I will take Holy Communion once I have been baptized. I can be baptized at any age if I feel the call.

After Baptism, the next step in becoming a full member of the Catholic Church is to make your first Holy Communion. Communion is the ceremony in which we share bread and wine as the body and blood of Jesus Christ. I made my first Communion when I was seven years old.

Preparation
During the year before I made my first Communion, I went to classes at church every two weeks to make sure I understood the meaning and the importance of the ceremony. We learned a lot about Jesus' teachings and discussed many of the stories in the Bible. We talked about God's hopes for us and about how we should live in a Christian way. Then, after many of these lessons, I was ready to make my first Communion.

Dressing for the service

The Communion took place one Sunday at my church at the morning Mass. Everyone dressed up specially for their first Communion. I wore a brand new navy blue suit. The girls all wore white dresses.

The First Communion

During the service, I was asked if I promised to attend Mass and whether I wished to make **confession** about anything that I had done that was wrong. Then I and the other children took the bread and wine as Jesus told his followers to do.

▲ At Communion the priest takes the bread in the form of a round wafer.

◀ The priest hands me a small wafer at my first Communion.

Marietta says:
When I made my first Communion I wore a long, white dress and I had a wreath on my head.

A Favourite Festival
Annie's story

▲ In church a crib shows how Jesus was born in the stable and people came to worship him.

One of my favourite church festivals is Christmas. This is when we celebrate the birth of Jesus. He was born about 2,000 years ago in Bethlehem. Christmas is one of the happiest times for Christians. I look forward to it because of the celebrations, presents, and the special services at our church.

Decorations

At Christmas time I help my parents decorate our house. We put up bright lights and a Christmas tree. I like the angel and the star that we put at the top of the tree, and all the other brightly coloured decorations that we hang on the branches. At the same time, we send Christmas cards wishing all our friends and family a merry Christmas and a happy new year.

Christmas services

At church there are different Christmas services. I usually go to a family service. The church is decorated with a tree, a crib and Christmas pictures. People act out the story of how Jesus was born in a stable because there was nowhere for his parents to stay. After he was born, some shepherds came to worship him and three wise men brought him gifts. At the end of the service, everyone is very happy, and people wish each other merry Christmas.

Marietta says:
My favourite Polish Christmas foods are carp and kutia, a desert made of wheat, honey, and fruits.

Our celebrations

On Christmas Day I'm always really excited. I get up extra early so that I can open my presents. I can't wait to take off the wrappings and see what my parents have given me. Our Christmas dinner is always really good. We have a goose with lots of different vegetables for the main course, and then my favourite – Christmas pudding!

Oliver says:
Every year we buy a tall Christmas tree and I help my family to decorate it.

◀ *We hang all kinds of glittering decorations on our tree.*

▼ *I open my presents in front of the tree. I tear off the paper as quickly as I can to find out what's in the parcel.*

People give presents to make Christmas special and to remind everyone that Christmas is about giving as well as receiving.

Glossary

acolyte Somone who assists in a church with duties such as lighting altar candles.

baptize To carry out the ceremony that makes a person a member of a Christian church. This is also called a Christening.

Bible The holy book of the Christian church.

carp A type of fish.

confession Telling someone what you have done wrong.

considerate To be kind and thoughtful towards others.

crucifixion A way of killing someone by hanging them on a cross.

disciples Followers of Jesus.

Easter The Christian festival that commemorates the Resurrection of Jesus Christ.

Episcopalians People who belong to the Episcopal or Anglican Church outside England.

festival A day that is important in religion and is celebrated every year.

God-parents People who promise to guide or help a newly baptized person in their religious life.

Gospel A reading from one of the first four books of the New Testament in the Bible.

Hallowed To be honoured as being holy.

Holy Week The week before Easter Sunday.

Joseph Husband of Mary, the mother of Jesus.

Kingdom Place where a king or queen rules, or where God rules as our king.

Mass Christian ritual in which bread and wine are taken as the body and blood of Christ.

Pope The head of the Roman Catholic Church.

prophets People whose sayings are inspired by God, or whom God enables to predict the future.

Protestants Members of churches that are separate from the Roman Catholic and Orthodox churches.

resurrection To rise from the dead.

rituals Religious ceremonies.

saints People who have lived an especially holy life and have been recognized by the church as having special status.

salvation Being saved from sin and its punishment.

sign of the cross A hand movement making the shape of a cross.

soul The invisible part of a person that goes on living once the person is dead.

spiritual Religious.

Stations of the Cross A series of pictures showing 14 events leading up to Jesus' crucifixion.

Sunday school Classes held to teach young people about religious belief.

Temptation When someone tempts or encourages someone else to do something wrong.

Trespasses Wrongdoings.

Further Information

Websites

BBC Religion and Ethics
www.bbc.co.uk/religion/religions/christianity

Church of England
www.churchofengland.org

Anglican Church of Australia
www.anglican.org.au

The Vatican (the Catholic Church)
http://w2.vatican.va/content/vatican/en.html

The Methodist Church
www.methodist.org.uk

Baptist churches in Great Britain
www.baptist.org.uk

Note to parents and teachers: Every effort has been made by the Publishers to ensure that these websites are suitable for children, that they are of the highest educational value, and that they contain no inappropriate or offensive material. However, because of the nature of the Internet, it is impossible to guarantee that the contents of these sites will not be altered. We strongly advise that Internet access is supervised by a responsible adult.

The Christian Year

The Christian year begins with the season of advent, which includes the four Sundays before Christmas. The most important dates in the year are those surrounding Easter. The exact date of Easter varies from year to year, but the festival always occurs in the Spring. Members of the Eastern Orthodox Churches celebrate the festivals on slightly different dates.

November/December
Advent Sunday
The Sunday closest to 30 November. This is the start of Advent, the lead-up to Christmas. The beginning of the church year.

25 December
Christmas
The day on which Christians celebrate the birth of Jesus Christ.

February
Shrove Tuesday
Traditionally the day on which people ate all the food they would not be able to eat during Lent. Shrove Tuesday is often called Pancake Day in Great Britain.

February

Ash Wednesday

The day after Shrove Tuesday and the first day of Lent. Lent marks the time Jesus spent in the wilderness and is a time of fasting and doing without luxuries.

March/April

Palm Sunday

The sixth and final Sunday of Lent, and the start of Holy Week. The day on which Jesus rode into Jerusalem.

March/April

Maundy Thursday

The day of the Last Supper, Jesus' final meal with his disciples.

March/April

Good Friday

The Friday before Easter. The day on which Jesus was crucified.

March/April

Easter Sunday

The day when Jesus rose from the dead. This is a day of thanksgiving and celebration for Christians.

April/May

Ascension Day

40 days after Easter. The day on which Jesus last appeared to his followers. After Acension Day, Jesus rose to heaven.

May

Pentecost or Whitsun

The seventh Sunday after Easter. This festival marks an event described in the Bible when the Holy Spirit appeared to the followers of Jesus in the form of tongues of flame.

Index